The Ultimate Cat Training Guide

Learn How to Train Your Cat and Solve Behaviour Problems

Table of Contents

Introduction

This book contains proven steps and strategies on how to train your cute, cuddly, yet rowdy cat.

Cats are loving and sweet animals; however, if you are planning to train it, you have to stop treating it and teaching it as if it is a dog. Cats are also intelligent and remarkable in their own way and we have to accept, appreciate and respect it.

In this book, we will first tackle and find out the dominant behaviours of cats. This is crucial in cat training so we have some basis on the way that they behave before, during, and after the training.

One of the chapters also clarifies the myth that cats, as opposed to dogs, cannot be trained. In fact, you can teach a cat the same trick that you teach to a dog. You just need more patience and creativity.

We will also talk about the possibilities and difference of training an older cat from a kitten. This is important for you to know because there are many older cat that are up for adoption and they need a loving family to take them in. Every cat, young or old, deserves a good life.

After that, we will identify the things that you need so we can finally get started with the training and then, we will tackle litter box training. We will also talk about why, at some point, your cat suddenly seems to forget what you taught it about housebreaking.

The topic of scratching and biting will also be tackled. We will not only find out what it is, we will also look at the reasons why cats bite and scratch. We will end the chapter by enumerating the step-by-step training so your cat will stop the unnecessary biting and scratching.

In the last chapters, we will tackle claw trimming. This may seem simple, but trust me; it is not always easy as it looks. After that, we will get to the hardest part which is training your cat to grow accustomed to bathing. Do not despair; there is a way to deal with it.

Lastly, we will talk about how you can keep your cat out of specific furniture without having to inflict pain or scare it. We have all that information in this book and much, much more!

Everything You Need to Know About Cats

The elegant walk, the silent and mysterious behaviour, the suddenly playful attitude that abruptly stops, and the nonstop snobbery... These traits surely describe any cat in the world. Despite the general snobbish attitude, there are still people who would pick them anytime over man's known best friend, the dogs.

What's not to love about these dainty, elegant animals?

They are effortlessly cute and haunting at the same time. Also, even though they usually ignore their humans, we can never deny the outburst of affection that they give us whenever they feel like it is the best time for cuddling.

None of us are born with knowing anything. Throughout life, we learn something new constantly and expand our knowledge. A lover of animals and responsible owner are not the same thing. At least 50% of cases, animal lovers do not act as responsible owners of their pets. Precisely because of that kind "animal lovers", the animals suffer the most.

Cat, also known as the domestic cat or house cat, is a small carnivorous mammal of the genus Felis. It is believed that their ancestor was the African wild cat. Cats living in close connection with people have been doing so for at least since 9,500 years ago. There are many different types of cats, some of which are tailless or hairless, as a result of mutations. The same is the reason why there are cats in different colors. There are also short-haired and long-haired cats. Cats are, by nature, the exact opposite of dogs. Unlike dogs, cats are stubborn and willful. They will often that they'll register your calling, but will not turn around and it

will come to cuddle only when they want. They are skilled predators and are very smart. They communicate by voice (meowing), spinning, snorting, spitting, and with a hundred other voices and body signals, such as the position of the tail, ears and hair.

An adult cat from nose to the tall is long about 60 cm. While their tail is about 25 cm long. A cat on average, weights between 2.5 and 7 kilos, although some species, such as the Maine Coon can reach over 11 kilos. In most cases cats get overweight, because of "overeating". This is very unhealthy for the cat, and should be prevented, proper nutrition and exercise (playing) which is especially true for cats that live indoors. Household cats live on average between 14 and 20 years, although the oldest cat lived up to 36 years. Domestic cats live longer if you do not get out of the home often. Cats that live exclusively in the street and at the same time are an intact/non-castrated, live much shorter - males up to 3 years, females up to 5 years.

Most cats have raised ears, while those with lowered ears are rare. When frightened or angry, a cat reacts with a snort, a growl, and sways ears back. Cat will also scrunch ears back when they're having fun and playing with other cats.

Cats gain strength by sleeping more than most animals, especially as they grow up. During the day, they usually sleep 12-16 hours. Some cats can sleep as many as 20 hours in 24 hours. Because of their nocturnal nature, in the evening, an increased hyperactivity in cats happens and desire to play. Temperament of the cats varies and depends on the type of cat and social factors. Shorthair cats are usually thinner and more active than the long-haired. Normal body temperature of cats is between 38-39°C.

Feline pulse is between 140-220 beats per minute and depends on how excited the cat is.

The widespread belief that the cat always lands on its feet, is true, but not in every case. During the fall, cat reflexively turns its body and corrects the posture by using its highly developed sense of balance and flexibility. It is always corrected in the same direction, if there is time for it, during the fall. (This only applies to cats that have tails). The tail, cats use for balancing during the fall. It happened that some cats fell from the fifth floor and survived, while some fell from the second and received fatal injuries. The reason for this is that in the later example, the cat didn't have time to position its body and land safely. Cats can cast their claws in different lengths, depending on whether they would use them to defend themselves or climb.

Feline night vision is superior to most living beings, not to mention humans. Cats are available to see different colors, but not as we do. Cats have a third eyelid, or a thin, transparent membrane that covers the eyes with. It can be seen at the moment when the cat opens their eyes, and when they're sleepy or happy. If it is a cat constantly shows the third eyelid, it may mean that the cat is sick and should be taken to the vet. Some types of cats (albino) and those with different eye color are often deaf.

If your cat has slimy eyes, which is often the case, it is likely that it caught an infection. Do not rinse eyes with herbal tea or any other alternative medicine solutions. Use only saline, boiled, lukewarm water. You can use for a couple of days, drops purchased exclusively in veterinary pharmacy. Make sure your cat does not have a respiratory infection, because in this case should not take any antibiotics. Also, make sure that your cat does not have a large infestation of intestinal parasites, because it can also be the cause of the leaking nose and eyes watering.

Cats can hear sounds of very high frequency, even higher than dogs. The sense of smell in cats is 14 times stronger than in humans. Whiskers help the cat about navigation and the sense of touch. It is believed that the cat cannot rely on their mustache when they find themselves in the mist. Also, the whiskers help them to keep balance. By looking at cat's whiskers, you can see their mood. When they are pointing forward, that means that the cat is inquisitive and friendly, but when they are relaxed and dropping down, it means the cat is aggressive or tries to defend itself.

Cats cannot taste sugary foods due to a defect in the gene for the reception of sweetness. Domestic cats are very good predators as they're, by nature, carnivore animals. They often bring their owner "trophies" like mice or bugs. The motive is not completely clear, but when we reflect that our cats are seen as part of the pack, it is considered that they wish to contribute to feeding the pack. Someone claims that they do this as a sort of gratitude. Cat definitely wants to be praised for their symbolic contribution to the group, and the motive can be to want to share the loot with the rest of the pack. You do not need to scream and heighten the tone because you saw a mouse, a bird, a cockroach, or anything else. Just quietly get the loot, praise your cat and forgive her.

Cat tongue has sharp creases, suitable for scraping the meat off the bone, but also cleaning their fur. It is common to cats in their meat diet occasionally bring small amounts of grass or herbs. When the cat is licking their fur, the stomach might accumulate some of the hair, forming a ball. In the wild, a cat eats a "cat grass" to induce vomiting, and release the accumulated balls of hair. Domestic cat does not have that privilege, so the cat grass should be purchased or a type of paste, which will form something like a lubricant and will help the cat lubricate the digestive system, so that hair is digested and removed through excrement.

Cats like to eat mainly raw meat, because it has a nutritional value that they need. Give them fresh mean, examined for human consumption, at least occasionally. Of course, raw meat brings a risk of infection with parasites, and it is necessary to regularly treat the cat against internal parasites.

Cat can eat only cat food. A combination of granules with occasional soft foods might be the perfect thing. It is a balanced diet with which you will never go wrong. With the help of the granules, cat removes the accumulated plaque on the teeth and thereby cleans its teeth, which should ideally be washed with the help of humans. When eating dry food – granules, cat will require a lot more fresh water than when eating soft wet food.

Occasionally deed the cat with vitamin pills to maintain their good immunity and to make them resistant to disease. You do not have to give it to them all the time, but for a healthy cat, once a week is more than enough. Mash thee pills into powder, mix with a little water, and give the cat directly into the mouth with a syringe (without needle – of course). Some cats love the flavor of these pills, so try it to offer them as a food, in small doses. If the cat has a weaker immunity or is sick, have at least 7 consecutive days of feeding them with 3 -4 tablets.

It is well known that cats like chewing grass, leaves, or the houseplants to remove stomach pains. Some houseplants are harmful to them, even deadly. Lily can lead to fatal kidney damage, Philodendron for them is also toxic, as well as a large number of other plants. Onion, garlic and chocolate, can be of a mortal danger to many cats. Cats also do not like the smell of citrus fruits (lemon, orange, etc.).

Cats can be picky in food, and one of the biggest misconceptions in most cats is that cats like milk. The fact is completely different. Often cats cannot stand the lactose in milk as it gives them diarrhea. The biggest mistake is to give milk or white bread dipped in milk, because the combination leads to diarrhea. White bread is not generally recommended; if you do not have any opportunity to feed the cat with cat food, give them rye. But, you should be aware that bread and many other foods for human consumption do not have the nutritive value for proper nutrition of cats.

A cat can be picky with food. Some cats to like human food, but it can be disastrous for them, for example - chocolate, because of the presence of the bromine. For cats, the best choice is cat food (granules in combination with human food), because these foods have a balanced amount of nutrients that will provide your cat with a better immunity and health, and even help it live longer.

Cats love to play with strings. They just cannot resist a rope dangling or dragging on the floor. If at the end of a rope is hooked a feather of birds, the experience is complete. If the cat swallows a piece of rope, thin wool or the like, it can lead to disease and often death. So, you always need to have them under the watchful eye of the owner. Therefore, some people in the game with a cat are using a laser with a red dot, but many were opposed to this because of the danger to the cat's eyes, although the main reason for this might be the loss of pleasure for the cat for successfully capturing the object. Due to the lack of understanding why they cannot catch the laser beam, the cat may become irritable and shaky, so it is not recommended playing with laser more than a few minutes.

Many cats like to play with small balls and even to run after them when they're thrown away. They like to be everywhere and a variety of boxes and containers makes a great deal of fun for the cat. During the game, you do not have to use small items that may accidentally get swallowed by the cat. Also, do not use any items that are not made for cats' playing, like pens, lighters, etc. If you gave them to the cat, be sure that you will never find the place where they left them.

Cats are Independent Creatures

I can never stress it enough, cats are independent creatures. They have a big inclination to do whatever they want. It may appear appalling and rude to you, but cats have an attitude of choosing to ignore you just because.

Sadly, there's nothing you can do to change their attitude.

However, learning to dance with your cat's attitude is another story. Cats are intelligent and you need to be more intelligent than them so you could control them. Making a cat obey you is like double-crossing the devil; you have to fool it into submission without it realizing what is happening.

Cats are not clingy creatures and they do not often cling to humans too. A normal cat will suddenly walk away from you if it starts feeling too much attention. If your cat unusually craves for attention, something is wrong. If this happens, you might want to check around for objects or events that cause stress or pain to your cats like a soiled litter box, illness, or a noticeable change in the house. Watch for small changes and signs as they are good clues to what is happening to your cat. If you still cannot figure it out, consult your cat's veterinary.

Cats are Naturally Clean Animals

Cats do not like dirt. While their bodily wastes are foul-smelling, it does not automatically make them dirty animals. There are many signs that will surely tell you about their cleanliness.

Cats are known for their purity. Cats are clean animals that clean themselves by licking their fur. Their saliva is a powerful cleaning agent, but in some people can cause allergies. Many cats enjoy to clean people or other cats. Many cats occasionally cough up (regain) ball of accumulated fur piled up in their stomachs. Long-haired cats are more prone to it. Cat, for this reason, should be brushed regularly, and remove the excess hair, cats should be combed regularly. Cats are not necessary in need to bathe, except in exceptional cases. Cats fed with high-quality cat food, regularly treated for fleas and internal parasites will have a healthy shiny coat and will not smell.

Cats defecate in a container with sand or other loose material. Their container should always be free of excrement. A bowl of sand must be sufficiently distant from the vessel with food and water; otherwise the cat may refuse to go into near it. The cat bathroom must be the place where they can always go.

Also, the cat needs something that will sharpen their claws. Cats that occasionally go out of the house, should not have their claws cuts, because in this case, the cat will be completely unprotected from all sorts of danger. When ripping claw of the house-only cats, care should be taken not to damage the vein, which is located within the claws.

Cats are the creatures that communicate mostly by body language, voice and smells. The scents are used directly, but from a great distance. The smells secreted by the sebaceous and sweat glands are transmitted by rubbing, scratching of objects, plants or people. Non-castrated males mark territory by spraying urine that is mixed with sex hormones. They spray it even at the apartment, where they reside, and the smell of urine is terribly unbearable.

Cats are territorial animals, which are linked to a certain territory, but also have their established habits. They do not like you to move their tableware or toilet, as they find thinks like that very stressful. Therefore, it often happens that a stressed cat exhibits strange behavior or even starts defecating outside of the vessel.

Cats are Routine Lovers

If you are considering taking a feline in as a lovely addition to your family, you have to start treating it as true part of the family before it even steps on your door's threshold.

Being observant and being a lover of routine comes together, and if your cat can talk, he will surely tell you that.

While small changes do not exactly stress you, it might be a different story for your cat. Your cat will surely notice the coming of a baby, house expansion, a new and large appliance or furniture, a visitor, redecorating your house and even moving his or her litter box to the next room. Your cat will notice it and will surely react.

Now, if you start noticing your cat use an unusual place to toilet, he is not annoying you. He is reacting like that because it is causing stress and confusion to him. It is good to prepare your cat for the coming changes by slowly introducing to him the sounds and smells until he or she understands that this addition will not harm him or her.

Knowing these information will help build a fundamental knowledge to your cat's behaviour that may appear puzzling to you at times. If you want to own a cat or you already own one, think like them and you will never go wrong.

How to Choose the Best Cat for You?

With or without a pedigree, long-haired or short-haired, male or female, kitten or adult cat – for every type of cat, there should be a different approach. When choosing a kitten or a cat, it is very important that you consider certain aspects of their lifestyle in order to obtain a cat that will be the best fit. Below are some questions that it would be desirable to ask yourself before making a decision.

Grown up cat or kitten?

Kittens tend to have more energy, are more curious and require more attention, while adult cats are generally quieter and prefer to curl up in a warm place. Adult cats can be the perfect pet for you if you are a person who likes to be sitting in the evening in front of the TV. Adult cats still have plenty of years ahead of him and can develop a character that will make them the ideal pet for you. Kittens can be a good choice if you have enough time to devote to them through play and interaction.

Some older cats can suffer from the effects of stress due to the new kitten or another adult in the home. It is important to take into account the character of the existing pets in your home and their level of tolerance towards other animals. Consider purchasing a slightly older kitten or young adult cat that has already been properly socialized and will be easier to fit into your home. It is very important if the household has children, that they completely understands how to properly treat a kitten. We suggest reading books about kittens before bedtime or joint viewing content related to this topic on the Internet. This will help all family members and cats to get used to each other.

While long-haired cats bring a more exotic appearance, they require daily combing to avoid tangles and painful nodules. Shorthairs also require brushing, but not so often. Sometimes it is good to comb the hair sufficiently to remove dead hair and those hairs that are about to be dropped.

The longhair Persian cats require careful attention to untangle comb every day. The hair is then brushed and ventilated. In short, prostrate hairs like those of Siamese cats need a lot of combing. Use a soft brush every week for medium length hair cats like Maine Coon cat, for example. The same applies to short coat with undercoat, as in the case of exotic shorthair cats.

There are cats of different colors - plain colored (yellow, black, silver, cream, gray), with markings on the coat (tabby, calico or tortoiseshell), both types which are of variety of races, both domestic and purebred. Pedigree cat, born from pairing of individual cats selected by the breeders, and properly socialized brings guaranteed morphological criteria that are set out in the breed standard. The same is true for their main character traits.

There is a selection of various cat breeds from elegant cats like Abyssinian cat, full of curves like British Shorthair, to majestic and peaceful, like the Maine Coon. Different breeds of cats offer such diversity that really worth to gather detailed information about it. Felinology clubs, exhibitions and breeders are well placed to good information. Going to a cat show is an ideal opportunity to learn a lot about the diversity and beauty of all types of cats in one place, with a chance to talk live with the present breeders.

When it comes to domestic cats, although it is difficult to know their ancestors, monitoring how they develop individual character traits has its advantages. In addition, by adopting a kitten of domestic cat, with a responsible ownership, you will participate directly in solving the problem of abandoned animals. And most importantly - save the life of a live being.

Advice for future cat owners

Although there is a well-known story about cats having nine lives, we will focus on how to keep your cat safe and healthy. In front of you are the answers to the questions with which every cat owner encounters, sooner or later. It is scientifically proven that cats can reduce stress and blood pressure of their owners. If you decide to bring your cat to your home, be aware that they will be spending the next ten years with you.

You have decided to buy or adopt a cat, but how to choose the right one? Siamese cats are known to be the loudest domestic cats and if you like peace and quiet, forget about them. Persian cats are demanding, because of their long hair. Kittens are cute and hard to resist, but keep in mind that it is easier to educate an adult cat. In the end, it all boils down to time, love and desire to indulge your pet.

It seems that every breed of cat can be the right choice, but only if you train it properly. Cats should not eat the same thing as you. Are you going to your cat to prepare meals or buy prepared foods intended for cats, it is your choice. It is important that the food is intended for cats, to avoid possible diseases, such as obesity or lack of certain vitamins.

Cats are naturally curious and there is little chance that the little kitten will not find itself in a million of potentially hazardous situation. That is why you need to prepare the apartment before their arrival. It involves isolating jacks and cables, as well as making a careful selection of toys. A hank looks like the coolest toy for every cat; however, the ball of yarn can strangle a cat. In addition, if the cat eats a piece of wool, it may cause diarrhea or even vomiting.

Going to the vet on regular basis is required; especially if you notice that the cat behaves differently. Cats can spend a long and happy life, but only if you treat them properly. Nutrition and regular check of the ears, nose, and fur are prerequisites for your cat to be with you as long as possible. Follow the advices discussed in this eBook and your cat will become a very important part of your life.

Can We Really Train Cats?

When someone mentions the words *training a pet*, we usually picture dogs sitting, rolling, doing their *business* in the comfort room, while sitting on the toilet seat, and similar things. However, did you also know that we can train cats too?

Contrary to popular belief, it is possible to train cats provided you add a little extra *kick* in the method that you use with dogs. By *kick*, I mean extra delicious treats and creativity.

Cats Do Not Respond to Negative Reinforcement

Spanking, kicking or other forms of inflicting some pain or scaring will never be good for your cat. It applies to all the animals you handle and train. While it makes them follow your orders *temporarily*, it still instils fear in them that can cause your cats to forget everything that you have taught them.

Negative reinforcement does not need admission to everyone else around you to correct it. You know what you are doing and how you do it. If you think that your temper or treatment towards your cat is starting to get uncontrollable or your cat is showing signs of distress, time to change it for good.

However, it is still best to not wait for your cat to show signs of distress as it will take time to correct this error before you see your cat act normal again.

Also, it would be good to keep in mind that training should only last for 10-15 minutes per day or you will risk making your cat despise the training or develop some sort of boredom with it.

Respect Your Cat's Independence and Individuality

Just like humans, cats have their own individuality as well. You will come to notice this individuality once your cat grows comfortable with you. Your cat comes in a package that contains independence and individuality. Your cat will never, ever part with these special traits. If you try to force your cat to give it up, you will surely end up getting scratched often.

The only step left to do is to learn to accept and respect your cat, snobbery, independence, playfulness, and all. Accept and respect your cat the way it deserves, you will get the same respect as well. Learning to live with your cat is the key to getting most out of its fun and loving personality.

How to train cats?

Cats are very intelligent animals, and no matter how old they are, they can learn to behave well. Like any other type of upbringing, the education of a cat must be based on the support, rewarding good behavior and pointing to the undesirable.

Maybe your cat already knows to behave well, when she comes to live with your family, but educating a cat is a process that never stops. A cat can quickly adopt bad habits, as well, and then it takes time until the issues are solved, especially if you tolerate such behavior for a while. However, bad behavior can be prevented with the right response - while training the cat, encourage it to for good behavior, and never mind when it misbehaves. Your kitten will quickly connect praise and reward with the right actions and will forget about the behavior, which you ignore.

When thinking about education, think about what you expect your cat to do, why would you want it to do that, and when will you will reward them. Cats are motivated mainly by food, but unfortunately this only works when they are hungry! However, it is good to find a treat that your cat particularly enjoys, which will help in their upbringing. Educating and disciplining cats is different from disciplining a dog, so you will not ask your cat to respond to commands such as "sit" or similar. However, you can teach your cat to respect some parts of your home, so that, for example, they known that they could not scratch furniture.

Cats are naturally clean animals and are looking for a litter box to defecate. Check the box every time to see if it is not accidentally moved. The litter box should be in a quiet place, away from food container, easily accessible and clean. If your cat is upset, and seek other places for defecation, you need to change the position of the box. The cat will quickly return to the habits of using the box, now when it's in the new place.

The following tips, tricks and techniques cover a variety of situations that most cat owners encounter. In dressage, first think about what you want to teach the cat to specify that this is done in the most effective way. The key part about cat training is consistency. No matter what you choose, make sure that you do it regularly; otherwise you will be sending your cat mixed signals, which will only further aggravate its development. Do not think that cat training finishes in 10 minutes.

Remember these tips to make your cat training easier:

1. Punishment means nothing to cats!

It is a fact! If you ever had a dog, you know that punishing him will help change their behavior. It does not bide well with cats. Do not waste your time - they will just sit there purring and then continue with the same behavior.

2. Corporal punishment is not an option.

Because the cat's body is so gentle, do not hit the cat. This means that when training your cat, you must use other methods to outwit and to achieve what you want. We do not doubt that you will succeed in doing so.

3. Use a form of positive reinforcement.

As you become a cat owner, you will find that it is difficult to "catch the cat in action" (rather wrongdoing). Therefore, it is much easier to reward your cat when you see good behavior. Make sure you have cat treats for your cat every time it does something good, such as using the sandbox.

4. Get plenty of toys.

You can buy them at the store for pets or make them yourself. Cats are often naughty, because they are bored. They are by nature predators. Remember the scene from the animated film "The Lion King" when small Simba learns lessons of stalking prey. When your cat goes down on the curtains and runs towards the wall, they're actually just practicing their predatory skills. Provide the cat with sufficient alternative materials to practice.

5. Make sure that the cat is "fun while you're gone".

If your cat is used to the society, it will quickly become bored with solitude and will slowly begin to destroy things while you are at work or when you there is no one at home for a long time.

6. Learn the value of the spray bottle of water.

In some cases, spraying a cat with water is enough to get their attention and stop the bad behavior. Really, all you need is a sprayer that you normally use to spray houseplants. When the cat starts to behave badly, you squirt. Soon, they'll know what is allowed and what not.

7. Blow in your cat's face.

It may sound strange, but it works. If your cat comes literally centimeters from your face and you want to teach it to keep a certain distance and give you some space, try this trick - simply blow into her face. The cat will startle and puzzle. Soon they will realize that they should not bother you anymore.

8. Make sure your cat has a room with a view.

You know the saying "curiosity killed the cat". It happens that the owner is angry because of something the cat has done, because of boredom. Many feline negative behaviors are associated with their curiosity. Make sure that your cat can sit on the windowsill and watch the birds flying outside or whatever's happening up there. If your windowsill is not big enough for the cat to sit there longer, try to expand the board.

9. Deal with the cat.

This might sound strange as a technique of training, but the more time you spend with your cat, the better you will be able to communicate with them. Cats definitely have well-developed communication skills. The better you know your cat and the better it knows you, it will be easier for you to read their thoughts. A lot easier for you to know what the cat is about to do. This goes both ways – the cat will know

when you disagree with what it does, by learning your body language.

10. You have more than one cat?

Cats will always fight over territory. If a fight starts while you are in the vicinity, the first thing you do is stop it. The best method is spraying water over the cats. Spray the aggressor, and avoid spraying the victim cat. After that, close the aggressor cat in another room. During this time, reward the cat who did not react, even though it was attacked.

These ideas are just a small part of the cat's upbringing. When you become more familiar with your cat, you will develop your communication. This can be done through speech - you're talking to it and she mews, but the language of the body is what matters the most. Soon you will discern the nuances of this form of communication and raising the cats will be easier than you thought.

The Difference of Training an Older Cat and a Kitten

Age does not matter to cat lovers, if they want to take a cat in their house old or young will do. However, how do they manage? If learning is possible with older humans, it is also possible with older cats. We only need extra patience for older cats, just like you would for older humans.

We know kittens are easier to train because they are like clean slates that you can write on without having to erase anything. It is acceptable if they fail or make accidents because they are young and they do not understand many things yet. The problem that you will have to deal with is their teeth and claws which are very sharp. Yikes!

Older cats may make you go excited especially if you see one in the adoption and you know that it is the right cat for you. It can also make you sceptic because it may have been through training already. There's also the chance that it

didn't go through any training and it will be difficult for you.

People think that if trying to teach a person to unlearn the bad things he has learned before is hard, what more to a cat who do not even know how to speak?

Still, do not let it hold you back. First, older cats are less aggressive unless they have been abused, injured, and given a hard time. If the cat you are planning to adopt has been through a hard time, you need tons of patience and understanding.

Just like any abused creature, cats will become defensive and they will respond either by running away from you quickly or hiss and try to scratch you. Cats that have undergone through hardship need an understanding owner to help it. You have to help it go back to interacting normally with people and other animals first before starting the behaviour training. It is hard but very rewarding once your cat is back to normal.

For normal yet older cats, you still need patience but not as much. Since you do not have any problems with it interacting with other creatures, you can start by helping it familiarize with its new surroundings first. Remember, cats know when their environment has changed. Let it grow comfortable a bit and start training it with the most important behaviour depending on how it already behaves as soon as it is comfortable in its new home.

If you notice your new cat uses every spot of your home as a toilet, address that first and train it for housebreaking. If it has a habit of chewing or scratching important or dangerous things in the house like electrical cords, address that first as it is more important than housebreaking.

Take note of your cat's attitude first before starting to train it. Chances are on its first arrival in your home, it will seem well-behaved and scared. Its true behaviour will show as soon as it feels comfortable already.

Cats can learn even tricks, but it is always important to finish and polish a certain training before moving on to another one. Do not train your cat or kitten with several behaviours or skills all at the same time because this will only cause him confusion and anxiety.

What You Will Need for Training

Finally deciding that you will train your cat is not the only thing you need to get the training started. You will have to arm yourself with the right attitude, materials, and proper place. If you have a family, you will also have to let them know about the training. Let us start!

The Right Attitude

I can never stress this enough, you will need lots of patience. If you are used to training a dog then you definitely have to condition yourself that training a kitten or an older cat as a slightly different story.

Your patience will be tested due to the cat's independence, just like a child who keeps on testing your patience because he is trying to do things on his own. Considering your cat as another child can help. If you treat your cat as just another pet or animal, chances are your patience won't be as lengthy as you would allow it when interacting with a child.

Make a List!

You are not going to the grocery, you are going to jot down all the behaviours and tricks that you want to teach your cat. If you still do not understand the necessity of making this list, let me tell what it is for. This list is not intended only for humanity's tendency to poor memory, but also for the benefit of your whole family.

This way, they can follow your cat's training so they can avoid having poor little kitty sit like a human on the sofa when you are actually teaching it to stop biting. The list, as the training goes on, will also help you arrange the training objectives by importance.

After your loving feline completes the whole list, you can give him or her a graduation treat for a big job well done.

Informing Your Family

Training a cat is like dieting. It won't be as effective and there is a huge chance of it backfiring if you are trying to have a balanced diet and everyone else on your family table is eating without care.

Cats can forget what you have taught them if you do not repeat the training regularly and if a family member accidentally juggles everything that you have installed into your cat's memory. It will cause confusion to the poor cat, you will end up mad, and both you and the cat will not achieve anything. Sad but true.

If you do not want this to happen, as soon as you have made up your mind about training your feline and have created a little list of what you are going to teach it, let your whole family know. This way, they will not accidentally mix up and mess what you have taught your cat. Letting them know about the training can also encourage them to join in and make the task easier.

Prepare Your Home

It might feel like Armageddon for some people because they even have to prepare their homes for training lovely little kitty, but trust me, you need this.

Get rid of things that will hinder your cat to reach his or her litter box. A really stressed cat who feels like his bladder is going to explode might cause an unwanted accident on your floor or carpet because something is blocking his litter box.

Stop moving that litter box and your furniture! Your cat will notice it and he will just get stressed from this endless furniture moving. If you do not want your cat to treat your whole home as though it is a giant litter box, stop moving your things.

There are dangerous zones and things for both kids and pets in every home. This is a spot that you do not want your cat to get into so block it, cover it, lock it, and do not make the big mistake of hiding a dangerous thing on a high place. Your child isn't tall and he or she cannot jump, but your cat can.

Materials That You Will Need

Just like any training, you will need materials. No, we do not need big equipment for cat training. I will make you a little list to make it more convenient for you.

- Laser Pen or Crumpled Paper

- Yarn

- Plastic Rod with Fishing Line Attached to Its End

- Catnip

- Scratch Pole (or cardboard box)

- Spray Bottle (filled with water)

- Yummy Quality Treats (not just dry cat treats)

- Litter

- Litter Box

- Double Sided Tape

The purpose of each material will be discussed further in the following chapters.

Using the Litter Box

The usual problem for cat owners is how to properly keep the litter box and make your cat use it constantly. Some of us who are lucky enough get to take home cats that are already litter trained, but for those who aren't too lucky, they will have to go through the whole training process to keep their homes from being a cat's entire urinal.

Where to Put the Litter Box

Do not place the litter box in closed or small spaces because this will only increase the chance of the lingering unpleasant smell. Put the litter box in an aerated space to let the air and smell circulate. Remember, cats do not like dirty or smelly things. If you want your cat to continue using the litter box, keep it smelling and looking clean.

Keeping the litter box in an open space helps if you have more than one cat. When cats are doing their business, they do not like getting interrupted. In cases where getting interrupted is unavoidable, cats prefer to leave the scene quickly. Providing them an open litter box placed in an open or aerated space will help them feel comfortable because it gives them the much-needed room for escape.

The litter box shouldn't be situated close to the feeding station. We don't eat in the lavatory and felines don't eat where they do their business either.

Be aware of physical restrictions your cat has, especially if it is an old cat. If he or she is having difficulty climbing the stairs, don't put the litter box in a place where your cat is required to go through so much climbing or walking. It will be troublesome for your cat and he might end up having an accident on your floor or carpet. Cats don't have strong bladder control so don't make them go through so much trouble only to get to a litter box.

How to Choose the Right Litter?

There is no such thing as a perfect litter because every cat has its own preference. Add in the preference of the cat owner and things get a little more complicated than it already is.

The best thing that you can do is to keep trying other brands and kinds of litter until you get to the one that you and your cat agree on.

Litter Box Training Proper

It would be good to observe your cat's behaviour first. Housebroken cats go straight to the litter box once they realize that nature is calling. It does not matter where you put the litter box provided there is nothing blocking it, they will surely find it!

For cats who aren't trained yet, it is best to know that most cats, particularly kittens, eliminate not long after waking up, after eating, and after activities. To help you anticipate when the cat will do its business, feed him or her at a regular time with a fixed amount of food.

1. Start by playing with it for ten to fifteen minutes then give its food.

2. Let your cat eat and clear up any scraps.

3. After your cat is done eating, it is time for another *light* playing session for ten minutes.

4. Make sure the litter box is prepared with fresh litter. Place your cat in the litter box and if there are any cloth, paper, or object that your cat had an accident with earlier, place it in the litter box to help it associate the smell with the litter box.

5. If your cat is not responding, try playing with the litter a bit to catch its attention and let it do its business.

If your cat goes out of the litter box and does its business on your floor or furniture, do not punish it. Simply lead your cat to its freshly made *accident and* let it sniff its *dirt*. Place the dirt and your cat in the litter box. Keep repeating this until your cat associates the smell of its dirt with the litter box. Once your cat understands what the litter box is for, it will go into the box on its own when it needs to do its business.

Also during the day, if your cat has been sleeping for more than two hours, gently wake your cat and call its attention to the litter box. Urge it to get in the litter box and praise it if it obeys you. If it does not follow, place it in the litter box and let it do its business. If it doesn't, it is completely fine so your cat will realize that the litter box is a clean place where it is safe to do their private business.

Always remember that every time your cat successfully obeys you, give a little treat and a little praise. This is not to spoil the cat, but to make it remember your training and realize that good things go hand in hand with good deeds.

Biting and Scratching

Most people avoid keeping cats in their homes especially when they have children around because of biting and scratching. What most people do not know is that cats can be trained to stop the unnecessary biting and scratching, especially at play time.

Why Do Cats Bite and Scratch?

There are socially normal cats and there are what we call territorial cats. While cats are exceptionally dominant to one another, they rarely act like this around humans. Territorial cats may stalk and attack unfamiliar individuals when they arrive. They see these individuals as gatecrashers who need to leave their territory.

Another reason for a cat to bite and scratch is when it is sitting or sleeping silently. Like I mentioned earlier, you have to learn to respect your cat's independence and individuality. Trying to carry or pet your cat when he or she is simply not in the mood may end up catastrophically. You will sure get bitten and scratched and you may end up hurting or scaring your feline companion.

Cats have their play time, eating time, cuddly time, and *me* time. If you see your cat eating or relaxing and you want to play with it, try to lure it with a roll of yarn. If it doesn't respond, it is best to leave it alone because it is not in the mood and you may only end up getting hurt. If it responds to your ball of yarn, lucky you!

Cats are also likely to bite and scratch in the middle of play time and it is not intended to hurt you. They are simply too happy they tend to forget that you are human. At times, they mistake their humans for cats who do not really mind getting playfully scratched or bitten.

Never use parts of your body as play toys like your finger, nose, mouth, hand, or feet. There are toys that you can use like yarn, a fishing line with a small toy attached to the end and a plastic rod on another end, laser pen, crumpled paper, boxes, and more. Using parts of your body as play toys is like indirectly teaching your cat to hurt you. If you have children, never permit your kid to tease your cat in any capacity.

Different cats will also show the *don't pet me any longer* attitude. They are known to endure petting for a certain span of time and afterward will suddenly yet playfully bite your hand.

Diversion is another common reason for a cat to bite and scratch. In case, two felines are swatting eeach other and you try to mediate, one or both cats may divert their resentment to you.

Training Proper

1. Never let your kids try and get your cat without grown-up supervision. Instruct your kids to handle your cat gently with one hand on his midsection behind his front legs, and the other hand on your cat's backside. In cases where your cat's legs are dangling, he will surely use his claws to keep himself from falling by embedding them in your skin. Avoid this by handling your cat properly.

2. Never use negative reinforcement as it will only cause stress and fear to your cat. It can also lead your cat to react violently.

3. When interacting or playing with your cat, always keep a spray bottle filled with water handy at all times. You will thank the bottle so much afterward.

4. In the middle of playing or cuddling and your cat suddenly bites or scratches you, let it know that you are hurt by saying *"Ouch!"* loudly, walk away and ignore your cat. For normal and sensitive cats, they will realize that fun time can be easily ruined by a scratch or a bite. This will teach them not to do it again in the future.

5. If your cat is proving to be specially stubborn and it continues to bite or scratch you in between playing or cuddling, say *"Ouch!"* and quickly sprays him or her with water using the spray bottle. Cats hate water, they hate getting wet and getting spritzed is no different. They will soon associate the unpleasant feeling of getting wet with biting and scratching. This will help them understand that scratching and biting is a big no when playing or cuddling.

Kneading

Making biscuits, massaging, kneading the pizza dough and many euphemisms are used to this adorable habit that cats have. Some suckle while kneading, some uses their claws as well, other cats use all four paws to knead, and some do not push their claws out. There are also various reasons why cats knead. Here are the following reasons for their adorable habit:

- Stretching in an Adorable Manner

- Marking or Leaving Their Scent on A Furniture or Their Loving Human

- Mating Season

- Your Cat is Happy (usually accompanied by sucking on the surface that they are kneading)

- Preparing Their Sleeping Spot

- Sign of Affection

However, no matter how adorable and sweet this gesture is, some people still do not appreciate getting their skins kneaded especially if their feline uses claws while kneading.

Now, what do you do to avoid getting kneaded and scratched at?

1. Do not interrupt your cat while kneading. Usually, when kneading is done by the cats to their humans, it is to show their sign of affection. Imagine hugging a friend and she tries to free herself from your hug? It hurts and your cat will feel hurt too.

2. If you see signs of kneading from your cat before it even happens (like your cat taking its position to properly knead on your back or leg), place a piece of thick fabric over your skin. This will act as your protection once your cat starts kneading with his or her claws out.

3. Enjoy the free mini massage!

Trimming the Claws

It is crucial to train your cat when it comes to trimming its claws before teaching it to bathe or you will end up like a raw dough from scratches. Cats usually react violently to claw trimming if they are not used to it, however declawing is not exactly advisable.

Declawing hurts and it is very inhumane. Imagine having your knuckles nearest to your nail removed just so you cannot cause damage to anyone using your nail? It is unreasonable. Some people prefer to have nail caps applied to their cat's nails, it is a better option but it still depends on you. Also, trimming happens before applying the nail cap. It means your cat really have to get comfortable having its claws trimmed.

What You Need?

- Cat Claw Clipper

- Towel or Cloth

- A Comfortable Chair

- Special Treats

What You Need to Do

1. Place the towel or cloth on your lap.

2. If your cat is new to this, you will want someone else to be around to help you out in case your cat needs someone else to hold him gently yet firmly.

3. Place your cat on your lap and pet him until he calms down.

4. Lift one of its front paws and begin massaging. This helps your cat calm down.

5. Gently press the pads of your cat's toe to extend the claw. Remember, their claws are retractable.

6. Give the claws a snip. If your cat tries to pull its paw, take a pause and massage again until he or she calms down then give one or two claws a snip. Remember to avoid the quick. Cutting the quick will cause bleeding and make your cat frightened.

7. Release the paw and give your cat a treat and repeat steps four to six for the other front paw.

Bathing

Cats and water are known enemies, however training your cat to bathe is not impossible at all. You simply have to start young, and if time is not on your side anymore, add more patience and yummy treats in your arsenal. You do not exactly need to teach your cats to love water, but if it is possible, go ahead! What you only need is to teach them to tolerate bathing and water.

What You Need:

- Bath Tub or Smaller Tub That Allows Your Cat to Walk

- Soft, Warm and Fluffy Towel

- Clothes (ones that you do not mind getting wet and covered with fur)

- Nail Clipper (for your cat)

What to Do: Water Exercise

This is only an exercise and we will not bathe your cat yet. It will take about 30 minutes to an hour. Do not hurry because you will teach your cat to be comfortable in the water.

1. Prepare a day before by clipping your cat or kitten's claws. This way, when you are ready to train it for bathing, a day has passed and the edges of its claws aren't as sharp anymore.

2. Place a soft, thick mat beside the tub because you will be kneeling for minutes. We prefer tub because it allows your cat to explore, plus it can accommodate your cat better than bathing it in the sink.

3. Make sure that warm water is prepared, a bit warmer than lukewarm because lukewarm feels cold for cats.

4. Bring the towel in the bathroom.

5. Enter the bathroom and bring your cat in. Assure it by petting it on the head or on its favourite spot. What's important is to make it realize that bathing is not scary and harmful.

6. Close the door let your cat explore and start filling the tub with an inch high of warm water. If you are using your faucet or shower head, set it at low to avoid frightening your cat with the sound of strong water coming out of it.

7. Check the warmth of the water and if you find it uncomfortable warm, simply add another inch of tap water to make it comfortable for your cat.

8. Set the cat in the tub and gently yet firmly hold it on its shoulders. It will try its best to come out of the tub, do not let it. Gently keep it in the tub and let it explore.

Talk to it to help calm its nerves and never give up until your cat becomes calm. There is a tendency that it will act calm and suddenly jump out so do not remove your hand from its shoulders until you see it walking around the tub in a calm manner. If it tenses and stops moving, it is not calm yet.

9. Once it grows calm to the water, sit in the tub with your cat. This is to help him or her calm down. Let it get close to you, but do not let it use you as a way out of the tub. Keep petting your cat until it settles in the tub.

10. Activate your shower head or faucet, but keep it low to fill the tub with warm water until it reaches the back of your cat. Your cat should not have a hard time keeping its head away from the water. Remember, the water should not be uncomfortably warm or it will scare your cat and your efforts will go down the drain.

11. Let it walk around and explore in the tub. Keep petting it if it shows signs of distress. Sometimes the stress is caused by the loud sound of water, if this is the case, set

the faucet or shower head to low. If your cat is still not calm, put the shower head under the water so it would not produce any sound.

12. If your cat is already calm, gently scoop water on its back. Be careful not to wet its head first.

13. Prepare the towel by warming it first in your dryer. Gently scoop your cat from the water and into the towel. Rub the towel on your cat if it is short-haired and squeeze if it is long-haired.

14. Keep talking to it and offer it a treat for a job well done. Repeat after two to three days to avoid having it forget what you just taught it.

If you think that your cat is still not that calm, two to three more sessions without shampoo or soap will not hurt because it will not damage your cat's skin or hair.

Restricted Places and Furniture

There are certain places or furniture in the house that you don't want your cat getting into. The reason is not only unwanted scratching, but also the possible harm that it can pose to your pet or family. While some people prefer to keep their cats out of the house to avoid this, some simply cannot part with their furry friends even at night.

Is There Any Choice?

Apart from keeping your pets out of the house, yes, there is another choice that will not emotionally hurt you or your pets. This is where double-sided adhesives or tapes come in. That and a good lung for laughing are the only things that you need.

Why Double-Sided Adhesives?

In case you are wondering, we are going to use these because cats do not like sticky things. What you are going to do is stick these sticky tapes on the furniture that you do not want your cat getting into.

You will see your cat try his or her best to get to it, fail, and just let go because it doesn't want its paws or claws get stuck repeatedly. Simple, right?

What If My Cat is Stubborn?

Spray it with water. However, treat this as a last resort because remember, you are teaching your cat to be comfortable in the water. Use sparingly.

Conclusion

I hope this book was able to help you to find various and friendlier ways to train your feline.

After teaching your cat or kitten the basic proper behaviour, you can move on to teaching it some tricks. However, always remember that you should finish and polish every behaviour before teaching it a new one. Also, do not forget to practice so your cat would not forget what you taught.

After all the hard work, do not forget to praise your cat and let it know that it did a good job. This is to encourage him or her to continue the good deeds.

Lastly, there will be times that your cat will seem like it has forgotten the training. Check for signs if it is stressed or sick and address it properly. Never forget your close relations with your cat because skills can be forgotten anytime, but your cat can always relearn it especially if it trusts you.

Remember, all relationships are built on love and trust. The same thought can be applied to your relationship with your loving feline.

Finally, if you enjoyed this book, then I'd like to ask you for a favor, would you be kind enough to leave a review for this book on Amazon? It'd be greatly appreciated!

Thank you and good luck!

Made in the USA
Las Vegas, NV
28 November 2022